Publisher's Note

A Word From Tony

I have been overwhelmed by the enthusiastic response United States General Statues Pamphlets has received since its inception. I am grateful and humbled by the support received from the staff and volunteers who lent their expertise by knocking on doors, making phone calls, sending mail or simply telling a friend.

I also want to thank the public for your overwhelming support which has allowed General Statues Pamphlet Publications to reach and exceed our first publication goals. In the end, the margin of victory was more than I could have ever expected when we started.

I am the executive publisher for Vision Books. We proudly publish the General Statues Pamphlets for the United States of America! These are 5 x 8 soft back pamphlets. No need to purchase the entire legal General Statues book. Just order the chapters that you need to serve your legal needs. Here are some examples:

Example 1): If you are incarcerated and you wanted to know if your trial process was handled in accordance with Civil procedure. You may want to order Pamphlets 1 & 2 which cover Civil Procedure.

Example 2): If you are incarcerated and you want to know about your criminal charges. You may want to order Pamphlet(s) 7,8,9,10 & 11.

Example 3): If you are incarcerated and you want to know about filing Habeas Corpus (How to get back into court?) You may want to order pamphlet 11.

This Publication is only a General Reference Guide. You may use it to purchase the General Statues Pamphlets that will serve your needs. There is an order form in the rear of this Pamphlet, just fill it out and we can bill a third party (mother, father, sister, brother, any relative or friend, etc.) on your behalf. This publication has been pre-paid by a family member, friend or clergy member.

If you do not need any General Statue Pamphlets, please refer this General Reference Guide to other individuals who may need assistance with their individual cases.

The enclosed guide is for the state of North Carolina. However, we publish General Statue Pamphlets for all 50 states. Just select your state from the order form on page 27 and after you receive your General Reference Guide for your state. You will be able to order the pamphlets of your choice.

It has also come to my attention that some pre-paid publications have not been delivered to the addressee. Please see the attached legal note.

We hope that you enjoy this General Reference Guide as much as we enjoyed putting it together. Let us know your thoughts and be sure to come visit us at www.usastatecodes.com or contact customer service at 980.729.3505

Best Wishes,

Tony Rivers Sr.
Executive Publisher

Vision Books
4325 Harris Boulevard, P.O. Box 42406,
Charlotte, NC 28215-1985
Tel. 980.729.3505   Office/Fax. 980.299.5965
Email. staff@visionbooks.org

Attn: General Statues Subscriber;

From the Office of the Publisher & Chief Editor

It has come to my attention that paid and pre-paid subscriptions of General Statues Pamphlets are not being delivered to the addressee. The enclosed copy of the General Reference Guide for the state of North Carolina is being tracked by the United States Postal Service (USPS), Washington, D.C. Division.

Federal Statutes and Regulations Relating to the Privacy and Security of Mail

The Postal Service has a long tradition of protecting both the cover and contents of mail. Mail protections are grounded in the 4th Amendment, federal criminal and civil statutes, postal statutes and regulations, and court decisions.

Title 18 of the U.S. Code (Crimes and Criminal Procedure) contains all federal criminal laws, including those enforced by the Postal Inspection Service. Title 39 (Postal Service) contains federal civil laws relating to the establishment of the Postal Service and its authority. Other relevant laws are also listed below. The major postal regulations protecting mail are contained in the USPS Administrative Support Manual, Domestic Mail Classification Schedule, Domestic Mail Manual, International Mail Manual, and Postal Operations Manual. Below are some of the more significant federal laws and regulations that pertain to the privacy and security of the mail.

It is a direct federal criminal violation of TITLE 18, U.S. Code: CRIMINAL PROCEDURE by any state or federal law enforcement officer, staff officer, corrections officer, prison

3

official, or any person, affiliate, or party thereto; too in any way, shape, form or any manner attempt to delay, steal, obstruct, or destroy any legal delivery of United States mail (i.e. magazines, legal books, from direct publishers.) These laws cover all 50 states. These laws protect mail delivery to all U.S. Citizens whether said citizens are incarcerated in any federal, state, city, county, or local municipality city jail, prison, halfway house, or any other institution or facility designed to house prisoners.

Section 1114: Protection of officers and employees of the United States
Section 1701: Obstruction of mails generally
Section 1702: Obstruction of correspondence
Section 1703: Delay or destruction of mail or newspapers
Section 1708: Theft or receipt of stolen mail matter generally
Section 1709: Theft of mail matter by officer or employee (of USPS)
Section 1716: Injurious articles as non-mail able
Section 3061: Investigative powers of Postal Service personnel

This is a pre-paid special edition copy of the General Reference Guide for the state of North Carolina. This subscription has been paid in advance by a friend, family member, or clergy. This General Reference Guide is only a guide to purchase North Carolina General Statues Pamphlets. In order to purchase North Carolina General Statues Pamphlets, you must fill out the enclosed order form located in the rear of the General Reference Guide and bill the subscription to any person of your choice (family member, friend, clergy, etc.) Do not remove this document from this magazine. It may only legally
be discarded by the addressee, period!

We ask that you the addressee (receiver of this mail) respond in writing to our agency at the herein described address to confirm that you did receive your paid subscription of the General Statues Reference Pamphlet, and or report any violations of this law. The legal staff at Vision Books will immediately report all reported violations to the Post Master General of the United States, and thereto the Federal Bureau of Investigations (FBI), and Secret Service having legal jurisdiction of investigation regarding violation of mail delivery laws.

On behalf of USA State Code Books, LLC. Thank you in advance for your support. Address any and all questions concerning this matter to USA State Code Books, LLC, Attn: Karl Winthers, PLLC, Attorney at Law, P.O. Box 42406, Charlotte, NC 28215-1985.

Sincerely,

Tony Rivers Sr.
Tony Rivers, Sr.
Publisher & Chief Editor

Cc: Patrick R. Donahoe, Post Master General; Gregory D. Cox, FBI-Special Agent in Charge Washington D.C. Bureau; & Guy Cottrell, Chief Postal Inspector (USPIS)

ABOUT THIS PUBLICATION

FOR SERVICE ASSISTANCE

Customer Service Department
1-980.729.3505

South Carolina Carolina General Assembly General Statues
is published by Vision Books in Charlotte, North Carolina.
Copyright 2018 by Vision Books. This book or parts thereof
may not be reproduced in any form, stored in a retrieval
system, or transmitted in any form by any means—electronic,
mechanical, photocopy, recording or otherwise—without prior
written permission of the publisher, except as provided by
United States of America copyright law.

The records required by U.S. Code 2257(a) through (c) and
the pertinent regulations 28 C.F.R. Cli. 1, Part 75 with respect
to this publication and all materials associated with such
records are maintained by USA State Code Books, LLC,
Publisher and available for review by Attorney General.

www.usastatecodes.com

Copyright © 2019 by Vision Books
All rights reserved!

ISBN (13) digit: 9781790829637

123-4-56789-09890-Paperback
123-4-56789-09891-Hardback

First Edition

120520181941

Printed in the United States of America

2019 EDITION

South Carolina General Assembly General Statues Reference Guide

(General Statutes of North Carolina)

Printed in conjunction with the Administration of the Courts

10

13

15

16

17

18

19

29

30

31

TITLE 29 – MORTGAGES AND OTHER LIENS

TITLE 30 – PUBLIC RECORDS

TITLE 31 – HOUSING AND REDEVELOPMENT

TITLE 32 – CONTRACTS AND AGENTS

34

36

37

39

40

41

43

44

45

46

47

48

TITLE 43 – SOCIAL SERVICES

49

53

54

55

**TITLE 48 – ENVIRONMENT PROTECTION AND
CONSERVATION**

59

60

63

64

66

67

68

South Carolina General Assembly
General Statues Reference Guide

Fax Orders:	1-980-299-5965
Phone Orders:	1-980-729-3505
Web Orders:	www.visionbooks.org
Mail Orders:	VISION BOOKS P.O. Box 42406 Charlotte, NC 28215-1985

Shipp To:
Name_____
Address_____
City_____State____Zip_____
Phone_____Fax_____
Email_____@_____

Bill To: We can bill a third party on your behalf.
Name_____
Address_____
City_____State_____Zip_____
Phone_____Fax_____
Email_____@_____

Pamphlet Number ($15.00 Each)	Qty	Total Cost
_____	_____	_____
_____	_____	_____
_____	_____	_____
_____	_____	_____
_____	_____	_____
_____	_____	_____
_____	_____	_____
Full Volume Set	92 Pamphlets	1,380.00

Free Shipping & Handling on Full Volume Orders
Add $1.00 Shipping & Handling per pamphlet $_____

Total Cost $_____

Thank you for your support. Management!

Order General Asembly General Reference Guides for other States

Fax Orders:	1-980-299-5965
Phone Orders:	1-980-729-3505
Web Orders:	www.visionbooks,org
Mail Orders:	VISION BOOKS P.O. Box 42406 Charlotte, NC 28215-1985

Shipp To:
Name_____
Address_____
City_____State____Zip_____
Phone_____Fax_____
Email_____@_____

Bill To: We can bill a third party on your behalf.
Name_____
_____
Address_____
_____
City_____State_____Zip

This order form is for a General Reference Guide Only. It will contain your pamphlet numbers and information on how to order your state's individual pamphlets.

Item	Qty	Total Cost

General Reference Guide for the state of:

_____ _____ $_____
Write your state name on this line.

($7.00 per pamphlet)

Add $1.00 Shipping & Handling per pamphlet $_____

Total Cost $_____

Thank you for your order. Management!

Did you enjoy this book?

Something you want to tell us? Please do, we'd like to hear your thoughts.

Send all written correspondence to:

Vision Books
P.O. Box 42406
Charlotte, NC 28215-1985
Email: staff@visionbooks.org

Phone Orders: 1-980-729-3505

E-mail Orders: www.visionbooks.org

Mail Orders: Vision Books
                          P.O. Box 42406
                          Charlotte, NC 28215-1985

www.ingramcontent.com/pod-product-compliance
Lightning Source LLC
Chambersburg PA
CBHW071230220526
45468CB00002B/788